Parents and the Bullying Problem

understanding and tackling bullying

A GUIDE FOR PARENTS AND FAMILIES

David Fitzgerald

BLACKHALL
Publishing

BLACKHALL PUBLISHING
26 Eustace Street
Dublin 2
Ireland
email: blackhall@tinet.ie

© David Fitzgerald, 1999

ISBN: 1 901657 74 4

A catalogue record for this book is available
from the British Library.

Printed in Ireland by
ColourBooks Ltd

Table of Contents

Acknowledgements ix

Introduction. xi

1   **Understanding bullying** 1

    What is it? 1

    The need for immediate action 2

    What can bullying involve? 3

2   **Bullying: adults must
      protect children** 5

    Bullying of any type is undeserved 5

    Myths about bullying 6

    Part of growing up ... forget it 9

    Unconditional support 10

    The reality of being bullied 11

3   **Bullying and leadership** 15

    *Can you distinguish between a
    strong personality, a leader
    and a bully?* 15

    Some parents' preferences 16

    *On bullying our message is
    loud and clear* 18

    *When physical violence is inflicted on
    children, the are likely to do
    the same to others* 19

    *A bully-free environment
    begins with me* 19

4   **Bullying in our schools** 21

*Do we know much about
   bullying in our schools?* 21

Some general findings 21

Other materials 26

5   **How do you know if your child
     is a bully?** 29

Once-offs are normally not bullying 29

Indicators to watch out for 29

Don't ignore it 31

Types of bullying 32

Denial is harmful 32

Problems encountered 34

Bullies lose out on life 35

Take action. 36

No excuses are acceptable 36

6   **Why do children and young
     people bully?** 39

7   **Why are some children more likely
     to be bullied than others?** 43

Factors which may be involved 43

8   **What can you as a parent do if
     your child is a bully?** 49

*Get them to step into their
   victim's shoes* 51

A difficult situation 52

Professional help 55

9 **Your child is being bullied: what can you do?** 57

Bullies can frighten people into silence 58

Some possible signs to watch out for..... 59

What can you do?.................................. 61

Your child is being bullied at school...... 61

Children need our encouragement and active support 62

Openness between parents and teachers..................................... 63

Being bullied outside the home 66

Speak with your child 70

Appendix 1 71
Samples of questionnaires for parents

Appendix 2 85
Recommended reference materials

Acknowledgements

I wish to express thanks to the many people who have supported me in writing this book. In particular I want to thank Ruby, my wife, for her advice, direction and patience. There are many colleagues in primary schools and secondary schools all over the country who have been very generous with their time and in sharing their expertise. My sincere thanks to them.

I wish to mention Elizabeth Quinn and her colleagues at The National Association for Parent Support and Finnoula Kilfeather from The National Parents' Council (Primary). Fr Dan O'Connor from The Education Secretariate in Archbishop's House, Dublin, Sr Eileen Randles from the CPSMA, Pat Diggins, Director of the Education Centre, Drumcrondra and Seamus Cannon and his colleagues in The Education Centre in Blackrock, who have all given me tremendous support over the years.

Last but not least my thanks to all in Scoil Mhuire, Shankill, my teaching colleagues, the parents, the pupils, the Board of Management, the secretary Pauleen Davy and its very able Chairperson, Fr Gerry Fleming.

Every good wish to all.
David Fitzgerald
March 1999

There will always be some bullying in schools, even the best run ones. Bullying spreads its wings and reaches out into other places outside the school classroom and playground. It rears its ugly head in many places, but particularly:

+ *in family homes*, where children can be bullied by an aggressive parent, or a spouse by a brutal partner. People can be hurt and humiliated, physically assaulted, psychologically battered and emotionally rejected within families;

+ *in the workplace*, where some workers prey on the vulnerabilities of their colleagues and some of the people in charge abuse their power by intimidating those who are under their supervision;

+ *on the field of play in games*, where, if unchecked, 'might is right';

+ *on housing estates*, where families may suffer ongoing harrassment and illtreatment and even have their possessions damaged or taken from them by aggressive, bullying neighbours.

Bullies and their Victims are Damaged

Some people suffer from being constantly bullied, and, nowadays, the seriousness of the problem, and the need to alleviate the suffering of so many victims of bullying, is undisputed. Bullying can have a devestating effect on the health and lives of people.

Thousands of children and adults suffer hurt, pain and humiliation at the hands of bullies both at home, outside the home and in school, on a daily basis. Some people who have been bullied become physically, socially and emotionally damaged - some are even driven to suicide. Bullies themselves, whose behaviour is not opposed, often have severe difficulties forming relationships and, unfortunately, may develop into dysfunctional adults, or even hardened thugs.

Unhealthy Attitudes

There were many strange, and in my opinion dangerous, beliefs about the effects of bullying, which has led to a high level of acceptance of children being bullied. One of the infamous phrases about bullying in second level schools was "it knocked the corners off you and prepared you for the good and the bad in life". Children were somehow considered to be better equipped than adults to accept physical hurt, verbal abuse, intimidation, name-calling and to live in an atmosphere of anxiety and fear. The action, or more correctly the inaction, of many adults posed many questions about the attitude of society and its ability to understand the feelings of others; particularly children and young people in bullying situations.

Thankfully, our society is becoming more aware of the serious consequences of unchecked bullying and more thought is being given to the damage done by all types of bullying behaviour and coercion. Serious and sustained attention is being given to research, policy development and action against bullying.

This Book

Nowadays, more and more questions have to be asked about the nature of bullying and what type of action could be suitable in preventing or countering it. This book is an attempt to answer some of these questions.

As a teacher and a parent, I have come across:

✦   many types of bullying situations;

✦   bullying situations which were handled well, and others which were handled badly;

✦   bullying situations which were extremely difficult to deal with;

✦   healthy, and not so healthy, attitudes towards bullying, bullies and victims;

✦   lives which were devestated by bullying in the home or in the community;

✦   good practice in schools for preventing and countering bullying.

I constantly meet parents and teachers looking for information on bullying and strategies for dealing with it and in this book I will share my experience with you and endeavour to support parents, teachers and school communities in keeping their communities "bully free".

Chapter 1

Understanding bullying

WHAT IS IT?

Bullying is far more than an isolated incident of aggression, which can occur between people, there is an aggressor who causes hurt or pain, and a victim, who suffers as a result and oppressive behaviour, which can continue unchecked for a long time.

Bullying causes wilful hurt which is unprovoked and repeated. The aggressor enjoys what is being done to the victim.

Bullying is, in my opinion, very aptly described by Rigby as:

> *Cruel, abusive behaviour which is persistent and pervasive and causes suffering to individuals which is severe and sustained.*[1]

The Department of Education's Guidelines on countering bullying defines bullying as "repeated aggression, verbal, psychological or physical, conducted by an individual or group against others".

Bullying is cruel behaviour which can cause physical, mental, psychological, emotional and quite often material harm to a person or group. It is premeditated, pervasive, persistent and

---

1.   Rigby, *Bullying in Schools* (1996).

cruel treatment, which is meant to hurt and harm, and is enjoyed by the bullying perpetrator. It is wilful, conscious abuse of an individual or group, which is inappropriate and unacceptable and, by its very nature, it demands that something be done about it immediately.

THE NEED FOR IMMEDIATE ACTION

It is of critical importance for adults in any community group (e.g. a family, school, local housing estate, workplace) to deal directly, deliberately and immediately with bullying incidents or suspected incidents. Bullying is wrong, and the task of bullies appears to be to make the lives of their victims unpleasant or even intolerable. Our task, as adults in a bullying situation is:

✦ first of all, to protect the victim, make sure that he/she is safe and feels safe;

✦ to analyse the behaviour of the bullying party(ies) and to get them, if possible, to change this behaviour;

✦ to try and ensure that the incident is not repeated.

In dealing with the bullying situation whatever action is taken aims to ensure that the bullying must stop immediately and that that those who are at risk are made safe. Further the social behaviour of the bully and the victim must be analysed and amended.[2]

---

2.   Besag, *Bullies and Victims in Schools* (1989).

We do not want to make the lives of bullies unpleasant if we can avoid it. However, it is important to remember that, irrespective of the social or economic circumstances of the bullies, all of their victims are innocent and undeserving of bullying treatment.

WHAT CAN BULLYING INVOLVE ?

Bullying can be physical, verbal, psychological or emotional and may be carried out by groups or an individual.[3]

Children who are bullied can be constantly subjected to:

+ unprovoked beatings;

+ being regularly kicked or punched;

+ continuous teasing;

+ physical harrassment in the form of shoving and pushing;

+ being called hurtful names;

+ being insulted or having their family insulted;

+ being verbally abused;

+ being threatened and intimidated by known aggressors, being bullied in school and out of school in their local neighbourhood.

+ having lies and false rumours spread about them;

+ having nasty notes written about them;

---

3.   INTO, *Discipline in the Primary School* (1993).

+ being isolated from groups and being left out of activities on purpose;

+ having their property damaged wilfully;

+ living in constant fear of something bad being done to them or their families;

+ being forced to hand over money or goods through fear and intimidation;

+ being made to feel bad about themselves because they are weak intellectually;

+ being teased and jeered because of their socio-economic, intellectual, mental, emotional or racial status;

These victims can suffer physically, mentally, emotionally and psychologically, and it is obvious that they need all of the protection which we can offer them.

Bullying causes stress, pain and hurt. It impairs an individual's ability to learn, to work, to play and to live at peace with themselves and others. It is intolerable for anyone to have to suffer such damaging behaviour and such cruel repeated oppression; it cannot be excused or justified.

Chapter 2

Bullying: adults must protect children

Our message about bullies, and bullying in our homes, schools and communities, has to be clear and unambigious. Bullying is a serious form of abuse against innocent individuals, which will not be tolerated and every action possible, and necessary, will be taken to stop it. It is ongoing, persistent, pervasive and cruel behaviour through which people, young and old, can be damaged and it has to be dealt with head-on.

BULLYING OF ANY TYPE IS UNDESERVED

It has been suggested that some people, because of characteristics that make them different or distinguish them from their peers, are more likely to be bullied than others. This is totally unacceptable as bullying of any type is undeserved and cannot be tolerated.

Children who are bullied suffer unfairly and undeservedly as a result of the actions of a bully and need the protection and support of the adults in their lives. There must not be any equivocation or ambivalence about bullying behaviour. It is wrong and it damages both the perpretator and the innocent victim.

Some of our children are more vulnerable and more easily hurt by bullying than others, and, as a result, we need to be even more vigilant with them to make their lives as secure and safe as possible. The vulnerable child, who is being picked on, may be baffled by what is happening and if he/she does not have our support they may believe that in some way they have brought the bullying on themselves and so feel guilty about what is happening. As parents, we can support our children by ackowledging and understanding the unfairness of bullying. Further, we cannot accept any excuse to allow our children to bully others or to be bullied themselves.

The actions of the bullying child and the sufferings of the innocent victim have to be attended to immediately and the bullying stopped in a determined and sure-footed manner. We will support children who are being bullied and help them recover from their ordeal, but the bullies themselves also need guidance to help them change their behaviour.

MYTHS ABOUT BULLYING

There are some myths among adults about bullying which often leave children vulnerable and unprotected. I have heard adults saying such things as:

"Bullying is part of growing up. It teaches them to deal with life."

"It is good for you. It toughens you up."

"Fight your own battles. Don't tell tales."

"Ignore it and it will go away. You must be doing something to bring it on yourself."

"Come on, stick up for yourself. You won't always have us around to stick up for you."

"I was bullied and it never did me any harm."

"You've got to be tough to survive in this world. You've got to take care of yourself."

"I never interfere in difficulties between children. They have to learn to sort out problems between themselves"

I have come across situations where children were subjected to severe and continuous harrassment by other children and when I brought it to the attention of the parents, particularly the parents of the 'aggressor', I was met with an inability to understand what was happening between the children. One or more of the statements/beliefs quoted above was trotted out and it was difficult to persuade them of their need to stop what was happening. These were good parents, who took good care of their children, but they had some type of mental block when it came to bullying.

We should carefully consider the following points.

+   If we act like this, what type of messages are we giving our children?

+   Are we leaving them to fend for themselves in the face of a bullying 'aggressor'?

✦   Are we asking children to rely on agg-
    ression, denial and cunning to defend
    themselves, or to submit to ill-treatment
    from those who are stronger than thems-
    elves?

✦   Have we as adults forgotten the pain and
    humiliation which a bully brought on us
    as a child?

✦   Have we forgotten the fear and great un-
    ease we felt when we were subjected to
    the behaviour and whims of a bully?

✦   Have we forgotten how let down we felt
    when we were not listened to by adults
    whom we trusted?

✦   Are we really refusing not to take children
    seriously and support them when they
    are in difficulties?

When we respond to children by using one of
the replies above, we are refusing to provide
protection and assistance. We are letting them
down and leaving them unprotected. We are
really saying to them:

> *It is your problem and you have to work your
> way out of it. Unless you come up with a
> solution and either tolerate what is happening
> or overcome the bully yourself, you will not
> have my approval.*

Can our good relationship with our children
sometimes depend on them not having problems?

PART OF GROWING UP: FORGET IT

Bullying, in spite of what some people would like us to believe, is not part of the rough and tumble of growing up or of ordinary everyday life. It cannot play a useful part in the child's normal development and does not as is sometimes suggested "help the child to toughen up and deal with life".

Bullying behaviour is all about gaining power over others, through violence of one type or another, and taking away their rights.

The bully derives pleasure and enjoys making others feel small. Bullies enjoy breaking people down:

✦ by hurting them;

✦ by physically beating them ... punching, grabbing, pushing and shoving, tripping;

✦ by vandalising or damaging their possessions;

✦ by blackmailing or intimidating them;

✦ by spreading malicious rumours or gossip about them;

✦ by taunting, mocking or jeering at them;

✦ by calling them cruel nicknames which causes serious personal hurt;

✦ by focussing on some physical difference or mannerism which the 'victim' possesses;

✦ by isolating them and making them feel that they are not wanted by their peers.

Researchers have found that bullying of any type is damaging to the psychological and physical well-being of an individual.

Bullies can create threatening atmospheres of fear and anxiety among their victims and make life a misery through their pervasive physical, psychological or verbal violence. Besag describes bullying as a "secretive behaviour"[1] which is kept secret in so far as possible from the eyes and ears of adults. Bullies know that their behaviour is unacceptable and most of their "work" is done in secret or at least away from the view of adults who would disapprove. They are usually clever and cunning, and it is generally very difficult to catch them in the act. Even bullies, who act in front of their peers in order to display their power or to win approval, want secrecy. They are often protected from adults finding out by a "conspiracy of silence"[2] which develops in the classroom or playground.

UNCONDITIONAL SUPPORT

Children have to be able to turn to adults unconditionally. They need to be able to express their feelings, their fears and their successes openly with adults.

If children cannot turn to adults without feeling shame, fear, or weakness then we fail them.

It is hardly good enough that a child believes that he/she has to overcome a bully to win an adult's approval.

---

1.   Besag, *Bullies and Victims* (1989).
2.   *Ibid.*

THE REALITY OF BEING BULLIED

Some years ago, I noticed that one of our fifth class girls appeared to be very unhappy and always seemed to be on her own in the school playground. When I asked her teacher about this she told me that the child was usually very quiet, but of late she seemed to have withdrawn into herself. She had spoken with the child and she had been told that she was worried about her Dad, who had lately lost his job. We agreed that I would approach the child in a situation away from the classroom.

As soon as I spoke to her, the child became very distressed. She insisted that there was nothing wrong with her. When I pursued the matter she told me that she couldn't tell me what was happening to her as she was afraid.

Eventually, having given her all types of assurances, she told me that she was very unhappy as one of her classmates was constantly making cutting remarks to her about her appearance and about her Dad being unemployed. She made fun of her in front of classmates and was constantly brushing up against her and bumping into her.

She told me that she had approached her parents, who were very caring and loving, but they had told her to ignore the other girl, keep away from her and it would pass. They did not seem to understand the seriousness of what was happening. As she spoke she became even more distressed and told me that there was nothing that could be done. She told me that her parents had problems between themselves and were experiencing financial difficulties as a result of which she felt it would not be fair to approach them again. They did not realise the seriousness of the child's situation and she felt totally on her own.

When I asked her why she had not approached her class teacher, or myself, she said that she had been threatened that if she did so she would be beaten up after school, and that the other children in the class would hate her for being a 'tell-tale'. The bully also threatened to injure her pet dog.

I immediately carried out a thorough investigation and through confidential conversations with other children in the class, I discovered that what I had been told was true. The other children had observed some of the bullying but as they had not seen the girl bullying others before they thought that there must have been something happening between the two girls and they did not want to get involved. Many of them also told me that they were afraid of the bully and her family.

When I interviewed 'the bully', I was quite shocked at the vehemence with which she denied what had been told to me. She was adamant that there had been a row between the two girls about name-calling and she claimed that, irrespective of what I had heard, she had been threatened and harrassed by ther accuser.

Eventually, as I was getting nowhere, I told her that I intended to bring in her parents and the parents of the girl who was allegedly being bullied. I knew her parents, who were very strict, and I was curious as to how she would react. She became deathly pale and pleaded with me not to take this action. She then owned up and admitted that she had been responsible. She admitted that she had picked on the other girl because they lived close to one another and she hated her for being a "goody goody"(her words!!). Further, she was constantly being compared unfavourably to her by her parents and she wanted to get her own back. Later, the three of us worked through the situation and the bullying stopped.

Not all cases have such a straightforward solution and some children will do everything they can to avoid admitting responsibility. Bullies often play on others' sensibilities and find the vulnerable spots which allow them to hurt their victims. They gain pleasure and satisfaction through oppressing, hurting or humiliating others and they are unable to empathise with the sufferings of others. The bully needs an excuse for the unwarranted behaviour and cannot afford to identify in any way with the victim.

Chapter 3
Bullying and leadership

CAN YOU DISTINGUISH BETWEEN A STRONG PERSONALITY, A LEADER AND A BULLY ?

Some children boss others about because they think that it is a sign of leadership. Adults, who are poor role models, may have encouraged children to think that people are important when they are in a position to order others around. They may be able to force others to bow to their will but it has little to do with leadership.

Leadership is about helping those less fortunate than ourselves by showing them what to do encouraging them, directing and leading them by our own example, to achieve success in life. Bullies, on the other hand, force others to obey them and do what they do not want to do. They use or abuse people for their enjoyment and, as it suits, they hurt them or damage them with impunity. Leadership supports and helps people feel positive about themselves, while bullying diminishes people and creates negative images in their minds about themselves.

Research and studies have shown that bullying damages children, adults and even whole communities. The seriousness of bullying, and the damage it can do, is undisputed. Yet many adults are reluctant to deal with it, and even try to deny the harm that it does. They appear to believe many of the 'myths' which exist about bullying and have an excuse to remain inactive and avoid doing anything about it. They are unable to distinguish between assertiveness, achieving, winning and bullying. They often envy and admire dominant personalities. To them, bullies often appear to be more successful in life than their more sedentary and passive counterparts. They admire and envy them for their seeming popularity and the power they hold.

SOME PARENTS' PREFERENCES

Some parents prefer their child to be aggressive and outgoing rather than quiet and easy-going.

Many parents consider dominant, aggressive, outgoing personalities to be a happier group of people. They consider bullies to be better able to take care of themselves and they believe that they will be better able to fend for themselves later on in life. They may even project that aggressive individuals will cause them as parents less problems later on. Where a highly competetive approach to academic, sporting or social success, which by intent makes others feel inferior or cause distress, is seen as acceptable behaviour bullying takes place. While there appears to be gain from this type of approach, the 'win at all costs' mentality is, at the end of the day, bad, and damaging for those who engage in it as well as for those who suffer because of it. The attitude of these type of parents "breeds complacency when it comes to dealing with the bully, and neglect when it comes to caring for the victim. It is based on the assumption that those who have an aggressive personality have a right to inherit the world. Little credit is given to the contribution made by less aggressive but more thoughtful personalities to the breadth and quality of our world."[1]

Guilty Feelings

Some parents may experience guilt about a child's bullying behaviour as it may be seen as a reflection on how the child was reared by them or even reflect their own personalities. The child may remind them of their own dominant, aggressive personality or that of their partner and they may feel responsible for the child's make-up and behaviour. They may then try to make excuses for the child's behaviour in order not to have to face up to the reality that the child they love is a bully or, in other cases, the victim of a bully.

In other cases, what a parent most admires in a child may be that very 'quality' which adds to the child's vulnerability and the possibility of them being picked on by bullies. Their outspokeness, their childish naievety, their love of dancing or music, their strength and physical prowess, their excellence at something or their gentleness and timidity may attract the attention of bullies.

---

1. Train, *The Bullying Problem* (1995).

ON BULLYING OUR MESSAGE IS LOUD AND CLEAR

Being a bully or being bullied can have devastating effects on the lives of our children if what is happening is allowed go unchecked. If action is not taken children can be given the message that bullying is an acceptable form of behaviour.

✦ Bullying is never deserved.

✦ Bullying is a serious form of abuse.

✦ Bullies are responsible for their behaviour.

✦ Bullies often try to frighten their victims into not telling.

✦ If you are being bullied and you tell us we will listen.

✦ We will act on what you tell us.

✦ Bullying will not be tolerated and allowed to continue.

✦ You have no reason to feel guilty.

✦ Bullying has no positive part to play in a child's development.

✦ Bullying must be brought out into the open.

✦ Bullying can lead to others being bullied if you keep it a secret.

✦ Bullying can lead to problems, often serious, for the bully and the victim in later life.

✦ Bullying is not something to be admired.

It is good to be helpful, kind and considerate to others. If you are stronger than others use your energy to help others, not to dominate them.

WHEN PYHSICAL VIOLENCE IS INFLICTED ON CHILDREN, THEY ARE LIKELY TO DO THE SAME TO OTHERS

Bullying is totally unacceptable behaviour and something to which us adults, particularly parents, must pay great attention. It is cowardly behaviour, is unprovoked and undeserved by those who have to suffer it. Bullying differs from the ordinary rough and tumble of everyday play and the child's normal process of development.

A BULLY-FREE ENVIRONMENT BEGINS WITH ME

Bullying behaviour causes pain, hurt and suffering which may have damaging effects throughout a person's life. Children ought always to be in a position to turn to adults unconditionally for help when they experience unprovoked, undeserved and cruel treatment at the hands of others.

Inaction by adults in the face of bullying is inexcusable. Whatever fears we may have, or whatever 'evils' we think may arise from our involvement and our actions to stop bullying, they cannot be worse than the 'evils' which befall children who are left unprotected against the cruel and callous treatment, which a bully may dole out.

An effective slogan to adopt and act on is:

"A bully free environment starts with me."

Chapter 4

Bullying in our schools?

DO WE KNOW MUCH ABOUT BULLYING IN OUR SCHOOLS?

Bullying has always been in our schools, and in other areas in the community. However, it did not become a public issue or an issue in UK or Irish schools until the mid to late-1980s. There was a fairly relaxed attitude towards it upto then. People generally tried to avoid having to deal with it if they could as it was considered to be part of living and growing up.

However, research has since clearly shown that:

+ a sizeable number of pupils suffer at the hands of bullies;

+ it causes both short and long-term damage;

+ school and community intervention to prevent or stop bullying does help.

SOME GENERAL FINDINGS

Scandinavia

It was commonly known that there was quite an amount of bullying in schools but little

research had been carried out into the incidence or consequences until the Scandinavians
led the way.

Research has been carried out in Norway
and Sweden since the 1970s. The two prominent figures were Heinneman in the 1970s
and, later, Dan Olweus, first working in Sweden and then in Norway. Olweus did much
work right through the 1970s and 1980s and
up to the present day. An English version of
*Aggression in the Schools: Bullies and Whipping
Boys* was published (in 1978) and, among many
other studies, he produced a very full study of
bullying in 1993 in *Bullying at School: What we
know and what we can do.*

In general, the researchers found out much
of what they learned about bullying in two ways:

+   studies asking teachers their views on
    the nature and incidence of bullying prob-
    lems in schools.

+   studies of children who are bullied, or
    are bullies, taking into account their
    general profiles, social backgrounds,
    attitudes and family influences.

A huge intervention campaign was undertaken
in Norway during 1983-1985, the results of
which began to come through in the late 1980s.

Some of the more general conclusions,
which have been drawn from this, and sub-
sequent research elsewhere, include:

+   Bullying by girls tends to be more
    indirect than boys.

+   Bullying is evenly divided betweeen one
    to one and that involving a larger group.

✦ The playground is the most likely place *for bullying in schools, but bullying can occur in classrooms, corridors and other locations.*[1]

About one half of pupils who admit to having been bullied and did not tell anyone about it.[2] This is very worrying and points to the fact that, unfortunately, many victims are either too scared or frightened to tell, are threatened so they do not tell, do not have the confidence to tell, or blame themselves for what has happened.

There is a marked difference between teachers perceptions of the incidence of bullying and actual bullying. This is due in the main to the hidden nature of some bullying and under-reporting.

Olweus[3] showed that boys, who were victims at school between the ages of 13 and 16, were, at 23, more likely to show depressive tendencies and suffer from low self-esteem.

Research into the effects of stress, which bullying causes, indicate that stressed, worried or upset pupils do not learn well, find it hard to concentrate or solve problems effectively.[4]

Bullying happens in nearly all schools and the consequences for the victim (and indeed

1. Rigby, *Bullying in Schools* (1997).

2. Rigby & Slee, *Manual for Peer Relations Questionnaire* (P&Q) p. 18.

3. Olweus, *Bullying at School: What we know and what we can do* (1993).

4. Turkel & Eth, "Psycho-pathological Response to Stress" in Arnold, *Childhood Stress* (1990).

the bully) can have long-term detrimental effects if support is not given.

Schools, which intervened to counter bullying, did succeed in reducing the incidence of bullying. Schools can do a considerable amount to reduce bullying.[5]

Since the 1980s, much research has been carried out in many countries including southern Australia, the UK and Ireland.

Australia

In southern Australia in the author's manual to *Peer Relations Questionnaire*,[6] the results of over 8,500 student questionnaires, from a wide variety of schools all over Australia, are described. An estimated 20 per cent of males and 18 per cent of females in the 8 to 17 age range, indicated that they were bullied weekly. Within these figures, the figure increased markedly when students entered secondary school. This certainly points to the need for work at the transition stage. The figures dropped at senior level in secondary school.

Statistics provided through KHL (Kids Help Line) in Australia suggested that the 10 to 14 age group has the most severe problems of bullying.

United Kingdom

In 1989 three important books appeared on the topic in the UK. They were:

✦   Tattum & Lane, *Bullying in Schools.*

---

5. Olweus, *op. cit.* and Roland & Munthe, *Bullying: An International Perspective* (1989).

6. Rigby & Slee, *op. cit.* (1995).

✦ Roland & Munthe, *Bullying, an International Perspective*.

✦ Besag, *Bullies and Victims in Schools*.

An excellent review on the research on bullying up to mid-1992 was carried out by Farrington in *Understanding Preventing Bullying*.

The Scottish Council for Research in Education produced two packs for circulation in schools *Action Against Bullying* (1992) and *Supporting Schools Against Bullying* (1993).

In 1990 the first large scale survey was carried out on 24 schools in Sheffield, known as the DFE Sheffield Anti-bullying Project. Its objective was to find out how pervasive bullying was and the typical age and gender differences within the phenomenon. The results confirmed the following.

✦ Bullying was extensive in schools.

Some 27 per cent of primary pupils reported being bullied 'sometimes' or more frequently and this included 10 per cent being bullied 'weekly' or more frequently. For secondary schools the figures were 10 per cent and 4 per cent respectively.

Twelve per cent admitted to bullying in primary schools and 4 per cent in secondary schools.

✦ Boys were found to bully more than girls.

The majority of incidents occurred in the playground. It was also shown amongst a host of interesting findings that school intervention had a positive impact on reducing bullying.

In Michelle Elliott's study of 4,000 5 to 16

year olds, which is included in *Bullying: a Practical Guide for Coping in Schools* (1991), she found that:

✦　　8 per cent of boys and 4 per cent of girls were severely bullied;

✦　　most bullies were one to two years older than their victims;

✦　　the most common advice to children from parents was to fight back. Parents preferred children to sort it out for themselves.

Ireland

In 1993/1994 Mona O'Moore, from the Trinity College Anti-bullying Unit, carried out a survey of bullying in primary and second level schools. The results to many people's surprise showed that 32 per cent of primary and 16 per cent of second level pupils had been bullied at some time. This survey is well worth reading and studying.

Guidelines for countering bullying were published by the Deparment of Education and Science in 1993 and all schools are requested to develop a policy on countering bullying behaviour.

. The 'Stay Safe Programme' (a child abuse prevention programme) was also introduced into schools in the early-1990s and the issue of bullying is handled very effectively. This programme adopts a three-way approach to preventing or tackling bullying, and involves schools, parents and pupils.

OTHER MATERIALS

There is much work presently being done and
there are agencies, which offer a variety of
leaflets, information sheets, videos, programmes, facilitators, seminars and even library
facilities. Most bookshops stock literature (fact
and fiction) on the subject.

Awareness of the prevalence of bullying, the
damage it causes and the need for information
and support from the community to counter
it, has led to a much more vigorous approach
towards reducing bullying and, where necessary, tackling it.

Chapter 5

How do you know if a child is a bully?

ONCE-OFFS ARE NORMALLY NOT BULLYING

In the normal life of children rows will break out, there will be the odd fight, names will be called, lies may be told about a peer or sibling, a child may damage another child's toy in anger, threats may be made or children may exclude another child from play. When children are corrected they generally agree to stop what is happening and relationships return more or less to normal. If, however, these type of incidents are repeated on a number of occasions and you are worried about what is happening, and you think that your child may be the bullying party, it is in a child's interest to investigate thoroughly and take whatever action is necessary.

INDICATORS TO WATCH OUT FOR

If you suspect, or are told, that a child is involved in bullying, what are the signs that you should look out for? What are the indicators that a child might be involved in bullying?

✦   Their attitude and behaviour towards the
    parents and other members of the family
    is generally, or has become, aggressive.
    They are sullen, secretive and difficult
    to approach.

✦   You have received a number of reports
    from school, or parents of other children,
    about fighting or bullying. Remember that
    schools or parents do not relish the pros-
    pect of having to inform you that your
    child is a bully.

✦   A child regularly has pens, sports gear,
    jewellery, clothes or money which cannot
    be accounted for and he/she cannot
    account for them.

✦   You have seen a particular child delib-
    erately hurt another child.

✦   You have evidence that a child has van-
    dalised or damaged someone else's
    possessions.

✦   A child constantly tells lies about his or
    her behaviour.

✦   When questioned about inappropriate
    behaviour, your child justifies it in the
    most strident and often surly terms and
    refuses to admit to doing anything wrong,
    or accepting any blame.

✦   Even when the wrongdoing is admitted,
    there is no sense of real remorse or no
    sense of empathy with the victim.

✦   A child appears to enjoy hurting others
    and seeing them suffer.

✦   A child tells stories or makes remarks
    about others in order to get them into

trouble. Subsequently you find out that they are untrue and even malicious.

✦ Other children, even within the class-room, are nervous or silent in the particular child's presence.

✦ He or she has changed friends and of late the behaviour is more aggressive and, at times, openly defiant.

✦ You discover that other children tell lies to protect a particular child.

If any, or all, of these things, or a mixture of them are happening constantly, and you see patterns of behaviour emerging you need to face up to the the possibility that a particular child may be a bully and may be engaged in bullying behaviour.

DON'T IGNORE IT

You may be worried and ashamed that a child could be involved in causing harm and inflicting pain and suffering, but choosing to ignore it will not make it go away. The reality is that if a child is bullying he or she is deliberately trying to hurt others and cause them pain and humiliation. Further it is very likely that he or she is gaining pleasure from doing so. It is premeditated, pervasive, persistent and cruel treatment which is meant to hurt and harm innocent victims who must be protected. The bullying child's behaviour has to change if he/she is to develop as a healthy emotional and social member of society.

In your child's interest it is important that you do not deny what is happening and that you take the necessary action to change the situation.

TYPES OF BULLYING

Bullying can take many forms.

+ **Physical:** beating, punching, grabbing, shoving and pushing, shoving and even injuring another child.

+ **Verbal:** cruel name-calling, verbal abuse, threatening with violence, jeering, mocking, taunting, insulting, spreading gossip or rumour or telling malicious lies.

+ **Psychological:** secretly damaging or vandalising another's possessions, threatening, telling untrue stories to another to create anxieties and fears, writing graffiti in public places to make someone an object of fun or shame, writing unsigned threatening or frightening notes or letters.

Much bullying is done in secret, by whispered threats, by threatening gestures, or by physical acts which are hidden from adults. Bullies can be devious clever and cunning, and are very capable of hiding their behaviour from adults who would be in a position to take action against them.

DENIAL IS HARMFUL

Over the years, I have come across all of these different types of bullying. I have investigated incidents, spent long periods of time breaking down denial by children, supported them in admitting and then helping them change their behaviour. In the majority of cases, we have been able to stop the bullying.

However, the worst scenario for me as a teacher has been where parents, after I had checked out incidents thoroughly, denied and refused to accept that their child was responsible. They tried to excuse their child's behaviour and generally tried to pin the blame on the child who was bullied, saying that he or she had provoked their child. They refused to face up to the fact that their child could be a bully and in some cases, expressed satisfaction and pride in the fact that he/she had been able to take care of themselves.

Very often it transpired that the parents had been bullied themselves and had not received any protection from adults and, as a result, accepted that it was best if children "fought their own battles". They believed mistakenly that aggression was the way to get what you wanted.

What they said and their reactions indicated to me in that they admired and envied dominant personalities and preferred their children to be aggressive and dominant. The view of life, of parents such as have, will be mirrored by children in their attitudes and behaviours and will have a detrimental effect on their lives. In reality, children are being told that aggression, inflicting fear and pain and intimidating others, is an acceptable way of relating to others.

PROBLEMS ENCOUNTERED

Research has shown that bullies, if their behaviour is allowed to go unchecked, experience many emotional and social problems particularly later in life.

+   They cannot relate to the sufferings of their victims and have little if any sense of empathy with them. They perceive the 'bullying' as normal, even though they know that we the adults consider it to be wrong and unacceptable. They have the greatest difficulty in taking responsibility for their behaviour and they will not do so if they can avoid it.

+   They find it difficult to have positive attitudes towards others and envy them their successes. They are deprived of one of the great joys of life which is the ability to celebrate one's own and other people's successes.

+   They consider thay the victim is always to blame. When they do not get their own way they blame others. Their reasoning and emotional response are faulty. They have a lot of anger in their lives, as they find it very difficult to accept defeat in any area and they feel bad about themselves. They personalise things to an extraordinary degree. This creates a constant source of conflict with others.

+   They feel unduly threatened by everything around them. Again, they personalise and cannot seperate situations from themselves and their own lives.

✦ They may have difficulty in forming, and maintaining, healthy relationships, particularly with the opposite sex. They are more likely to get involved in difficult and often aggressive or violent relationships.

✦ Research has shown that bullies are more likely to get involved in crime later on in life.

Train (in *The Bullying Problem*) points out that two of the main characteristics of bullies are:

(a) their need and desire for power and dominance of others which distorts relationships;

(b) their feeling of alienation from the world (both the openly, competitive aggressive bully and the cunning, secretive bully) and their resentment and feeling of hostility towards others.

Train also points to the adoption of obsessive behaviour and the developing of a sense of 'paranoia' among individuals who engage in bullying over a long period.

BULLIES LOSE OUT ON LIFE

The person who bullies loses out, both as a child and as an adult. They lack the capacity to behave in an appropriate manner in their communities. They lack the capacity to reach out and seek help or receive it at times in their lives when they may be experiencing emotional, social or other personal difficulties. If people are angry with others, they will not have the trust, openess or ability to relate to others, or to discuss their feelings, that is

necessary if we are to live comfortably as accepted members of society.

TAKE ACTION

Irrespective of what questions arise, or whatever reasons are given for the bullying, it is
important that you do not deny what is happening and that you take the necessary action to
change the situation.

You, the parent, are the expert on your own
child, and most of the help and support can be
given by you. However, if you consider that
you need extra help and support it is advisable
to approach your school, or your school medical
team, and be guided by them.

The bullying situation has to be tackled and
the child supported in admitting the bullying
and accepting responsibility for the behaviour.
This should be done in a decisive, but private,
manner. We want to avoid public humiliation
of the child. We want to stop the bullying and
when the behaviour changes we want to re-
affirm the child's worth in as many ways as
possible and, when the situation has been
dealt with, we move on.

NO EXCUSES ACCEPTABLE

There is no excuse for bullying and we must
not accept any. Bullying is all about causing
hurt to others. It is generally not a one-off
occurence, but it is repeated cruel treatment
and has ongoing, damaging effects on the
victim. The bully has a reason in his/her own

mind for what is happening and gains satisfaction from treating others badly. The bully will feel a sense of power through dominating others and not have the normal sense of empathy with a person who is suffering.

Chapter 6

Why do children and young people bully?

The reasons for children bullying can be many and varied and children of any age can be involved.

The pre-school child, who has been landed in an unknown group away from the security of the mother may take out his feelings of frustration on peers.

The 12 year old who finds the transition to second level too much for him or her can be filled with fear, apprehension and anxiety of failing. The child may decide to fail on his or her own terms, and engage in anti-social behaviour, such as bullying.

Children model the behaviour seen in the home, either observing violence or being subjected to it. When physical punishment is inflicted on children they are likely to do the same to children with whom they come in contact.

The poor relationship which some children have with their parent(s), can be reflected in the negative attitude which the child has towards other children and adults. Where a parent appears to reject the child and is negative towards him/her the child may, as a result, bully other children as he/she has developed a faulty response mechanism towards others.

Some children have a low sense of their

own value and worth. They feel they are failures and are angry with the world and act aggressively to gain attention, to feel power over others.

Some children are victims of bullies themselves at school or at play in their locality. They feel powerless and frustrated about the situation and, as a result of these bad feelings, they begin to bully others who are weaker than they are.

They bully to gain acceptance with their peers. In some gang situations, for both boys and girls, it is necessary 'to prove yourself' in order to be part of the gang.

Bullies can be jealous of other children, who appear to be more successful than they are, have more possessions or are more popular. Jealousy has been found to be one of the main reasons given by children for bullying, particularly those who have a low sense of self-worth. They feel that life has given them a bad deal.

Bullies lose out socially because they cannot enjoy others successes. They often become angry and resentful of others.

The behaviour of younger children can deteriorate if there is a new arrival in the family. They feel angry as their mother or father spend less time with them and give them less attention. They take it out on others in the family or, as sometimes happens, on the new arrival.

They know that they are physically strong and get a feeling of power from 'bossing' others around. Again they are probably copying behaviour they experience or observe in the home and/or in the community. They may even get some misguided, admiring approval from certain adults for their aggressive 'macho' behaviour.

Bullies may have some physical disability of which they are conscious but with which they have not come to terms. They feel different to other children and may even be jeered and taunted about their disability. They bully out of frustration and to feel power over others.

Because of a change in their family situation, the child may be under severe stress. The child feels alienated from the community and the bullying is a form of revenge. This change in behaviour is usually temporary and may be caused by:

✦ a parent's loss of employment and status perceived by the child;

✦ loss of the family home;

✦ a change of home and the loss of much that is familiar to the child;

✦ a death in the family or the death of a friend;

✦ the loss or death of a pet;

✦ alcoholism in the family;

✦ marriage breakdown;

✦ violence in the home;

✦ a parent or sibling in prison;

✦ poverty.

They are so insecure within themselves that they enjoy making others feel small and inflicting pain on them.

They are not used to taking turns, sharing, being part of a group, losing at any type of game or taking directions as to behaviour. They simply bully their way into getting what they want.

A child may be emotionally or mentally disturbed and as a consequence be unable to interact socially in an appropriate manner. This type of child may need medical and psychological assessment and then will need further support or treatment. The earlier the intervention is made the better, so that action can be taken to modify the behaviour.

Your child may have joined up with new friends who have a reputation for being difficult, and you might have heard that they have a reputation for causing trouble. Your child, to gain acceptance and win approval, may take on the behavioural characteristics of the gang. Is your child easily-led? They may be weak academically and are failing at school, and, as a consequence, they may feel bad about themselves, and could be inwardly angry and may be attempting to gain attention through aggression towards others.

Children may be victims of the ambivalence in attitudes among some adults about bullying. Some adults express pride and admiration when they see their child dominating other children in play. Some people have the mistaken belief that there are certain behavioural characteristics, such as bullying, which really do not harm people and are part of the normal process of growing up. Such misguided and ill-informed views encourage children to be aggressive - children absorb far more of their parents and other adults' values than they sometimes care to imagine.

Adults need to examine carefully their personal attitudes to bullying, if they are to be in a position to help children change their behaviour.

Chapter 7

Why are some children more likely to be bullied than others

FACTORS THAT MAY BE INVOLVED

Any pupil can be bullied, but some children are more at risk and prone to being bullied than others. Unfortunately, there are factors which may be used by the bully, and which may contribute to a child being more likely to be the innocent victim of a bully.

These factors can include the following.

✦ Being different in any obvious way to the general body of pupils in a class or school, e.g. having a physical disability, an unusual tone of voice, belonging to an ethnic or racial group, or even being timid.

✦ Lacking confidence and not being able to mix. This may result in name-calling or physical abuse.

✦ Being very clever. Other pupil's jealousy can result in them being called names like 'swot' or 'lick' and I have even heard of a child being upset because he was called 'teacher'. The child's possessions and work can also be damaged and vandalised by jealous peers.

+ Being very weak academically or having special educational needs. Children who are withdrawn for remedial work are often jeered. Name calling can occur and such names as 'thick', 'spa', 'dummy', 'header' and 'donkey' have caused upset to children and in some instances led to retaliation or severe distress.

+ Children from homes where there are problems can be vulnerable and taunted or jeered. A family member in jail, a parent who is a known alchoholic or drug-user, a relative with an obvious mental problem who sometimes acts in a bizarre manner in public.

+ An overprotective parent can focus unwarranted attention on their child and hurtful jeering and name calling can result e.g. Mammy's boy or girl, Mammy's pet, 'softie', 'sugar-puff'.

While we want to protect our children, we have to be careful that we do not draw unwanted attention to them. Teenagers are particularly sensitive about how adults relate to them in public. If your child asks you not to do something or say something in public think about it carefully. What is normal for adults may have a different meaning for the young person.

Children whose Hobbies are Different

Being a new boy or girl in the class or neighbourhood can cause a child to be bullied. This can be the result of another child being jealous of the attention, which the 'new pupil' is receiving, or because they are afraid that they will lose a friend to the new arrival.

Some children are bullied because of their hobbies, interests or pastimes. In one case with which I was involved, a boy who played hockey was mercilessly teased and taunted. The school which he attended did not have a tradition of boys playing hockey and the other boys considered it to be 'soft', a cissy's game and definitely not 'cool'. The boy in question was particularly talented at hockey and en-joyed the game. He had also been a talented football player but had not the time for both games. He was jeered about being afraid and soft.

The problem only came to light when he suddenly gave up hockey and refused to discuss why he had done so. The parents made some quiet enquiries and got to the bottom of the story. Working with the school, which took a sensitive but firm line, the issue was resolved and the boy returned to his hockey.

Children who have hobbies, which are not in line with the majority culture in a school, can become the objects of unwanted attention. They may be unjustly and without cause considered to be trying to make themselves different or to be 'snobbish'. The irony is that the very strength, talent or quality, which parents admire and promote in our children, may be the ones which cause them to be unfairly picked on.

Children's Physical Appearance

Having particular mannerisms, spontaneous physical facial movements or jerks, having prominent physical features (teeth, eyes, ears, nose, lips), wearing 'told-fashioned' clothing, being awkward or clumsy or being too small or too tall - any of these factors can lead to a child being bullied or picked on. At the teenage stage, in particular, young people are very sensitive about their appearance and their growth patterns. Personal remarks may provoke heightened reactions and if individuals or groups become aware of this heightened sensitivity they may play on it and it can result in bullying.

Children who are overweight can suffer terribly through name-calling, not being able to participate in some physical activities and being jeered as a consequence. They need plenty of support to recognise their worth and learn to accept themselves and not react to the taunting. They need to be helped to see such behaviour for what it really is - pathetic.

Sexual Undertones

Boys who do not participate in physical activities or team sports can be jeered about their sexual orientation and even considered to be reserved or 'snobbish'. Boys who are gentle are often considered by some of their peers to be effeminate or homosexual.

Many disparaging words dealing with sex and sexual orientation, which are used to hurt both boys and girls, have crept into pupil's language. Words such as 'queen', 'fairy', 'slag', 'slut', 'fag', 'bender' are used openly and need to be discussed in families and in schools.

Young people can be jeered because of their perceived lack of sexual experience and may feel pressure to become involved in, or brag about, supposed sexual activities merely to be part of the group.

Children who React Easily

The young person who becomes visibly upset and is very quick to react to jeering or name-calling may become the focus of attention of an individual bully or a group. He/she will be seen as a soft target and be seen as someone who 'is easy to wind up' and get going. Adults need to do everything possible to stop the bullies but the victim who is being so cruelly treated may also need special, or specialist, help. They will need to develop better responding skills, to boost their own self-esteem and to remain calm in stressful situations. While nobody has any right to bully them, these victims can make it easier for themselves if they know how to behave in a manner which does not attract the attention of a bully. While we cannot accept bullying it is advantageous to know how to leave a bullying situation or to avoid bringing the unwanted attention of bullies on to us.

Even Wearing Glasses!!

Having to wear glasses can cause major problems for some children and young people. Younger pupils have been known to break, hide or to purposely mislay their glasses rather than wear them. They do not want to wear them because of name-calling and jeering. Traditionally, glasses were associated with very studious people, with older people and with seriousness and dullness. Some comics and magazines still portray this image. It is advisable, if your child has to wear glasses, to talk to them beforehand - even the choice of frames can make a difference. There are fashionable frames available which may make the whole situation easier.

Schools and families working together can achieve a great deal in terms of developing effective stategies to combat bullying.

Children will suffer, be hurt, or even damaged because bullying is systematic and cruel behaviour. It is helpful to think of a family or a school as a community where everyone has equal rights, enjoys safety, feels free and lives and works in a helpful environment. Within this community, when bullies step over the line of normal behaviour, they are guilty of abuse and the community should take appropriate action.

Chapter 8

What can you, as a parent, do if your child is a bully?

If your child has grown up in an atmosphere where almost all topics can be discussed, irrespective of how difficult it is for them or you, then it is likely that your child, whether as victim or bully, will discuss a bullying situation with you. The quality of the relationship between you, as parent, and your child will be a big determining factor in your child's decision whether or not to tell you about a situation.

There are no hard and set rules for dealing with a bullying situation, as each is different. However, we must all adhere to one rule, which, in my opinion, is paramount:

If you suspect or know that your child is being bullied, or is bullying, you must investigate it thoroughly and act immediately.

Having said this you will find that a number of different types of situations may arise and all will demand different approaches.

1. You suspect, or have been told, that your child is bullying and you investigate. If you can get the child to admit to bullying and to agree to stop the bullying behaviour all will be well. Then, if apologies are necessary, you can help your child to make them, and start afresh.

2. If you get a report from a school that your child is bullying a few points are worth noting.

    ✦ Remember that teachers are not happy about having to tell you that your child is a bully.

    ✦ Question your child as soon as possible and try to unravel the facts.

    ✦ Visit the school with the answers to the questions about the incident.

    ✦ If the situation is clear-cut, sort it out quickly and amicably.

    ✦ If there have been mistakes made and your child is not to blame give this information to the teacher.

    ✦ One way or another, work with the school to sort out the situation.

    ✦ At all times, indicate that you want your child to accept responsibility for his/her own behaviour.

    ✦ Continue the investigation and try to work together to get to the bottom of what is alleged to have happened. Work with the school, and ensure that you are familiar with the code of discipline and, in particular, the anti-bullying code. Make it clear to the school that you do not want, nor will you accept, your child's behaviour.

3. Talking with your child. All of the time keep the lines of communication open with your child. Talk to and listen to him or her. Try, now and again, to manoeuvre the conversation towards bullying or telling you what is happening in their lives. It helps to try to get them to understand the point of view of their victim.

GET THEM TO STEP INTO
THEIR VICTIM'S SHOES

Ask the bully the following questions.

✦ What would it feel like for you to be made to do things out of fear?

✦ How would you feel if you were called names which hurt your feelings?

✦ How would you feel if someone bigger was constantly pushing you around?

✦ How would you feel if people made jokes about you and made fun of you in front of others?

✦ How would you feel if you were left out of games or groups?

It can help to bring up a situation where they were made to feel bad by someone else.

✦ Can they remember how they felt?

✦ Was it good for them?

✦ Why do they think the other person did it to them?

✦ Did they want it to be stopped?

✦ What did they do to stop it or who did they tell?

  You might talk about a smaller brother or sister being bullied.

✦ How would you feel if they were being bullied?

✦ How would he/she feel about it?

✦ What would you do about it?

You might describe how you were bullied and discuss how you felt and what you did to stop it. This would give your child an opportunity to listen to your thoughts and hear you express your feelings about bullying. You need not over moralise. You probably will not see an immediate change, but generally, it results in the seed being sown for a change in attitude and behaviour.

Schools and parents working together can, and do, sort out the majority of these problems. However, please bear in mind that solving these types of problems often takes time.

A DIFFICULT SITUATION

If you suspect, from different things around your child and his/her behaviour, that there is bullying taking place but you cannot get proof or an admission, then you could be facing a difficult, but usually a solvable, situation. You will have to look at many areas of your child's life to try to come up with a solution.

You can ask yourself some questions. For example: Have there been changes in the family or school situation which could have adversely affected your child? A death, an illness, a change in family circumstances, a change of house, a family conflict? It is important that you try to pinpoint any changes which might be relevant and take them into account. They may provide the answers to your worrying questions about your child. Remember, while circumstances may have an effect on the child, he/she still has ultimate responsibility for his/her own behaviour. However, if you find reasons which may have contributed to your child's bad behaviour then you can work on ways to make it easier for your child to accept responsibility for the behaviour, to change and to cope.

If, on the other hand, having looked at different angles to the problem, and having spoken with your child, he/she denies bullying and you still have suspicions, you will have to go further.

As parents at times like these, we are often at a loss as to what to do. We may be afraid that if we take action the results may make a bad situation worse. We ask ourselves what we can do to change the situation without damaging our child, particularly our child's reputation. If we have to go to the school to clear up matters, or if we have to approach a neighbour or a neighbour's child, our child may lose friends and he/she will definitely be angry with us for exposure to public shame. It may be necessary to seek outside help.

If we cannot sort out the problem ourselves we may even feel ashamed or foolish for having to approach others. These feelings are understandable, but have to be put aside. As parents we cannot turn a blind eye to bullying because of the damage our enquiries might cause. If you suspect or know that your child is bullying you must investigate it thoroughly and immediately, because you can be certain it will damage your child and your child's development if it is allowed to continue. There is no way around this. If you can sort out the problem yourself that is fine, but if you cannot you will have to look for support and help, wherever you need to.

You can spend time with your children, encourage them to share their thoughts and feelings, do what you can, but seek advice, assistance or support if you need it. Be prepared to share your concerns with others and listen to their advice and accept their support if you think it can help. Take whatever action you think is necessary.

If you can talk with your spouse or partner, other members of the family, a trusted relative or neighbour, then do so. Discuss your suspicions, share your concerns and seek their support and ideas. Another person will be able to see the situation in a different light or confirm your own suspicions and feelings about your child's behaviour. You may decide to talk with a trusted neighbour or friend who you consider would understand this type of situation and again share your concerns. Coming from outside the home they could throw new light upon the situation. Others can listen, understand and present a different perspective.

You May Have to Go to the School

If necessary, and it is recommended, go privately and speak with the authorities in the school. Make an appointment with the class teacher or principal and speak with them confidentially and, if necessary, make arrangements to co-operate and monitor the situation.

Most schools welcome parents who are open with them and they will generally have experience in dealing with similiar bullying situations. The teachers may also have noticed a change in behaviour and be perplexed by it and your visit will be welcome. Together you may decide what action to take next, at home and at school, and move the problem towards a solution. You can tell your child later. It is generally not wise to do so before, as it can leave the bullying individual feeling more cornered and angry and he/she may decide to dig their heels in further.

If, eventually, your child admits to the behaviour you can agree on a punishment. Speak to your child calmly and sure-footedly and spell out the facts as you see them. Enter into a discussion about the bullying: why it happened and what should happen next.

If the school is imposing a punishment do not duplicate it at home. However, be very clear about your disapproval of the bullying and what your expectations are for the future. Be firm but fair, and use the opportunity to encourage your child to share thoughts and feelings with you in the future. Try to start with a clean sheet and leave the past behind you both. Start afresh.

If the child feels that he/she has been treated unfairly, exposed to public ridicule or whatever, damage will be caused if you do not work it out between you. So it is worth spending time on this situation, listening, discussing and explaining. We want our child to come out stronger from this 'bad' situation and at all times we want to rehabilitate, not annihilate.

PROFESSIONAL HELP

If, however, you are unable to sort out a situation do not hesitate to consult with professionals, who are specially trained to deal with bullies and victims. They can work with bullies on a one to one basis or even in groups and provide effective personal treatment programmes.

Chapter 9

Your child is being bullied: what can you do?

In most cases, if there is a child being bullied in school, in the home or somewhere outside the home, the intervention of the teachers and parents can stop the bullying.

You can find situations:

✦ where older brothers or sisters are defending younger siblings over-zealously;

✦ involving an ongoing row where one child blames another for getting them into trouble;

✦ of pure and simple dislike of one child by another;

✦ where a child becomes the butt of bullying behaviour, cruel teasing or jokes of a gang or class;

✦ where a mistaken view of what a joke is which has caused a child to be regularly made to feel bad.

These situations in themselves, if not checked and stopped, can be very serious but once tackled firmly, fairly and decisively they generally stop.

However, other situations can be more problematic and can occur at any age from 2 to 18 years. Recognising and pinpointing the 'bullying problem' can be difficult because your child has not told you about it and even though you strongly suspect it is happening he/she strongly denies it when questioned.

BULLIES CAN FRIGHTEN
VICTIMS INTO SILENCE

It is important to remember that bullies work by using fear and intimidation and get what they want through frightening others. They do not want their actions to be known by adults, who might be in a position to take action against them, so they often threaten their victims with injury to themselves, their property, or their relatives if they 'rat' on them. A bully can exert extraordinary power over a victim to force them to remain silent.

Remember that bullies do not abide by the normal rules of behaviour. They can be clever and vicious in frightening others into:

✦   not telling or seeking support from adults;

✦   becoming passive to please them;

✦   thinking that they have to accept what is being doled out, to be resigned to their fate, or face even worse treatment;

✦   feeling that, irrespective of what they do, the bully will be able to get back at them;

✦   into feeling that they deserve to be bullied. They cause them to believe that something about themselves, their families or something they are doing causes them to be bullied. They make the victim feel guilty and feel bad about himself or herself.

It is important to remember that, irrespective of how open and close the communication is between you and your child, if he/she is being bullied he/she may be too frightened to tell you. The terror, which the bully has instilled into his/her mind, will prevent disclosure being made to you by your child.

SOME POSSIBLE SIGNS TO WATCH OUT FOR

If your child is being bullied it can manifest itself in many ways:

+ through a change in behaviour;

+ a change in play habits;

+ moodiness;

+ a general demeanour and appearance of unhappiness;

+ outburts of anger;

+ through, almost, total withdrawal into himself or herself.

If a child is being hurt and subjected to pain and humiliation outside the home, and feels unable to do anything about it, he/she may react negatively, either aggressively or over passively, towards the family and take out their frustrations in the home.

You may suspect that bullying is to blame for these changes in behaviour, but you are unable to put a finger on what is happening. You may not have not observed anything that should cause your child's fear, anxiety or worry. You may have noticed that your child's behaviour and moods have changed over a short period of time and he/she while visibly anxious or upset insists that everything is fine.

This change in your child may be exemplified by:

+ unhappiness in school and a reluctance to get up in the mornings;

+ wanting to be collected in the evenings and appearing to be very apprehensive leaving school;

+ often complaining about feeling sick in the mornings without any visible physical signs;

+ a deterioration in the child's standard of work, accompanied by a lessening in interest in schoolwork;

+ being liable to become upset or cry for the smallest reason;

+ being reluctant to go out and play as was usual;

+ being unusually negative about issues;

+ making comments and statements which downgrade himself/herself;

+ appearing to be generally unhappy;

+ being late home from school without plausible reasons;

+ cuts and/or bruises on the body and explanations that are not really credible;

+ school books, sport's gear or toys go missing regularly and can't be accounted for;

+ developing a sudden interest in self-defence magazines or activities and wanting to join a club. When you talk about this you may get hints as to what is happening, whether it is a leisure interest or a means of striking back. This happens particularly in the 15-18 age range;

+ becoming uneasy or unneccessarily upset when particular peers at school are mentioned.

You find that your child is not his or her normal self and you are asking yourself why is this happening, trying to put the pieces together and trying to get to the bottom of it. Having looked at what is happening, you may decide that your child is being bullied and it is time to take action.

WHAT CAN YOU DO ?

Remember, your own views about bullying will determine how you respond to a bullying situation and how you deal with it. Do you see bullying for what it is and the damage it causes? Or have you some tolerance of bullies and bullying?

There are different ways of dealing with a bullying situation but the one approach which is sure to fail is to avoid facing it or to tacitly accept it. It will not just go away.

YOUR CHILD IS BEING
BULLIED AT SCHOOL

If you are reasonably sure that your child is being bullied at school, do not hesitate to go to the school and discuss the matter with the class teachers and/or the headteacher. Teachers may have noticed a deterioration in your child's behaviour and performance and will welcome your visit. Give your picture of what you think is happening and listen to what the teacher thinks. If the picture is not clear, you may have to leave some time to work together and to decide on how best to monitor and tackle the problem.

Irrespective of what plan you decide on the contact between home and school will give both sides the opportunity to look at what is happening and see the change in your child's behaviour in a clearer and more informed way.

It is good if you can both decide to take every opportunity to listen to and build up the child's self-esteem. Bullying often causes children to feel that they have very little worth in comparison to others.

CHILDREN NEED OUR
ENCOURAGEMENT AND
ACTIVE SUPPORT

Even if you have given the message many times before, make sure that your children know, from your words and actions towards them, that you accept them in all situations and that you value them sharing their thoughts, their feelings, their fears and their successes with you. Concentrate, no matter how hard it is for you, on seeing the good qualities and positive strengths in your child. Help them in any way you can to become aware of these qualities and strengths.

We can support the child who is going through a difficult period if we:

✦ watch for opportunities to encourage the child to talk;

✦ make sure time is available to listen to the child if he/she wants to talk;

✦ praise them whenever possible, and be specific in this praise. As in most situations, children can see through general praise and children, who are under pressure, generally do not like to be publicly singled out;

✦ tell him/her what you think of what they have done;

✦ try to ignore bad behaviour, if possible;

✦ focus on their strengths and talents;

✦ if you can get them to talk to you about their work or themselves encourage them to do so as this may be the avenue into solving the bullying problem;

✦ reassure them of their self-worth.

OPENESS BETWEEN PARENTS AND TEACHERS

Rest assured it will not be the first time that the school has encountered and dealt with a situation like yours. Teachers are, generally, experienced in dealing with this type of situation and their ability to resolve it is much increased if they have parents working with them.

One note of caution. It is important that the teacher has all of the information that you have relating to the incident.

Have there been previous incidents between these particular children, or between other members of the family?

Is there a history of your child being involved in bullying situations?

Irrespective of your child's history he/she has a right to be defended against bullying, but it complicates matters if a teacher is told by other teachers, or parents, rather than yourself, something about your own child's past, which they consider to be relevant. I have often found that, when I went to investigate an incident, there was an ongoing fued between the two families, or that the parents had met about the incident in question and there had been serious disagreement.

If there is anything related to the incident, which the teacher should know, tell him/her in confidence. While schools try to ensure that bullying does not take place, if the problems between parents or families are brought into the school by children it can make situations very difficult to sort out.

Sometimes, with the best will in the world it will not be possible for the school to sort out a particular bullying situation but rest assurred that markers will have been laid down for the bully about future conduct.

If, on the other hand, you were the complainant and the school finds that your child was partly responsible, or even the ringleader, be prepared to accept this. Be prepared to admit that your information was not correct and meet your child with this new information. Tell the school that you do not want another child to have to shoulder the responsibility for your child's bad behaviour and you expect that he/she will have to accept whatever disciplinary measures apply. In any situation like this the aim must be for all to be accountable and to take responsibility for their own behaviour.

What you want is the bullying behaviour to stop and stay stopped and you will play your part. If you have not been given the correct information by your child or others, admit it and get down to the serious business of sorting out the problem with the new information. Teachers will understand what has happened, and remember you are both on the same side trying to get to the bottom of what is happening.

Be Realistic

It would be extraordinary for a school not to look into a bullying incident and not to take action when they determine correctly who is responsible. The culprit may not be punished in the manner in which you would have wished, but you can be certain that the school will do everything it sees fit to do and can safely do to stop the bullying. In a school, one can often be certain that particular individuals were involved in an incident, but it may not be possible to get the admissions, or the proof, to take action which the teachers would consider appropriate. However, schools can do much to warn bullies and assure them that they will be on the alert to notice and take action on any future bullying behaviour.

Problematic?

Where children are being protected by 'difficult' or 'aggressive' parents getting the bully to admit their behaviour can be almost impossible. The same situation arises outside the school where parents defend their children, who are bullying, or even facilitate children in lying about their behaviour. It is very frustrating for the parent of the victim but equally so for teachers, who can only do their best by working together.

The danger in this type of situation is adults getting caught up in a new problem which arises out of their own behaviour. They become angry with each other and the main bullying problem may become the secondary one. Communication breaks down and nothing is resolved.

As parents we must not allow ourselves to be diverted away from our main objective which is to have the bullying stopped. Do not allow yourself to be drawn into angry or confrontational situations. The parent who will not allow their child to take responsibility for the bullying welcomes an angry response and angry adults rarely sort out problems.

BEING BULLIED OUTSIDE THE HOME

If you know, or suspect, that your child is being bullied outside the home in a place other than school, you need, again, to investigate thoroughly to try to get to the source of your child's problem. Question your child thoroughly and have a clear picture of what happened.

If you know who the bullies are, you will have to decide on the best way of sorting out the problem. Try to check the situation with one of your child's friends or speak with some of the neighbouring parent's before you do anything. Try to confirm the truth of what your child has told you. You may also need to get some information about the bullying child or the family before you approach them.

You may decide to approach:

✦ some of your child's friends. Be careful not to accuse or threaten another child. It is often best to speak to their parents before approaching them.

✦ your child's teacher or the school principal. They may have noticed something or have some extra information about what is happening. Schools will not want children bullying each other, and they generally have experience in dealing with all types of bullying situations. You will find that if they can help they will.

✦ one or more of your neighbours whom you could trust. If the parent(s)of the child whom you suspect is considered to be difficult to communicate with then you will have to plan carefully how to inform them and to get them to respond positively. You may have to go to a person who is friendly with them and ask them to approach them.

You may be advised to accompany your child on different journeys during the day. You may be advised about the manner in which you should consider approaching the bully's family

or you may even have an offer of mediation.
While schools are in no way obliged to investigate incidents which occur outside the school
they are usually very helpful.

However, before you go to the school or
neighbours, if you know the bully's parents,
you should approach them, as they would
probably resent it if you were to approach the
school before approaching them.

Do not go directly and make an accusation,
as accusing someone of bullying is very serious
and bullying is a sensitive subject for many
parents. It is best to be sensitive to the fact
that the parents may be ashamed if they find
out that their child is a bully. Simply say that
there appears to be something going on between the children, and ask them if they have
noticed anything or been told anything. Say
that you do not know what is happening but
you think that your children may be fight-ing:
your child is upset and does not want to go
out to play and is reluctant to go to school. Do
not make any allegations or threats if your
hope is to create a situation where you can
sort the matter out in a mature, adult manner.

Then you will have to wait for the response
of the other parent and the conversation may
move towards an agreement, or not. The other
parent will need some time to speak with their
child, so do not make demands. The majority
of parents will not want their children to bully
but they will want to hear their child's side of
the story. It can create difficulties if you rush
the situation.

You can indicate that you would like to sort
out the situation as quickly as possible as your
child is upset and if you get the opportunity,
or if you find it necessary, point out that if

your own child is in any way responsible for what is happening he/she will accept responsibility. The aim is for all to be accountable and take responsibility for their own actions.

You can be courteous and friendly and yet assertive. You can indicate that you want the situation sorted out but do not make demands. You must not under any circumstances become angry. Make your point and indicate that you want to work together to pursue the problem until it is sorted out.

No Agreement

If you do not reach agreement, or receive a hostile reception, do not despair as you will have brought up the subject and looked for answers. Approaching parents and making them aware of your suspicions will generally be enough to get them to look into what has been happening. If you have gone to the trouble of going up to their house parents will recognise that you are serious and concerned.

If their response is hostile or threatening you must be firm, hold your ground and work towards getting a committment that what is happening will stop.

If the bullying continues, you may have to speak to the police and be advised by them. This may result in the police speaking with your child and the other child, but bullying is too serious and dangerous a matter to leave unattended. You may be advised to go to your solicitor and he/she will advise you on what action to take. Going to the police and/or a solicitor is not something that is done lightly, but in extreme cases there is no other option left if you are to protect your child and, in extreme cases, to protect your family and yourself.

SPEAK TO YOUR OWN CHILD

We can do much to alleviate the pain, terror, suffering and humiliation which bullying causes by listening to and supporting our children.

Be sure to speak with your own child while all of this is happening. Their emotional pain can be easily overlooked while you are trying your best to stop the bullying and ensure that it remains stopped.

Children who are anxious, frightened and worried need time to recognise that it will be good for them to tell you about what is happening. They may be fearful of something happening to themselves or even to you. They need reassurance that being bullied was not their fault, and that you are there to listen to them. They need to know that you consider it brave and courageous not to be frightened into keeping the bullying secret.

If they are feeling guilty, you need to hear it and support them in understanding their innocence and that the bullying was totally undeserved. They must know that bullies are responsibile for their own behaviour and it is bad for everyone if they are protected.

Children need opportunities to express their fears and, eventually, tell you how they feel about what has been done to them and how they feel about the bullying child. You can then reassure them that you understand how they feel because of what has been done to them and you are going to make sure that it does not happen again.

Appendix 1

Questionnaires: examining our own attitudes as parents

Listed below are a number of questionnaires designed to look at your attitudes towards bullying behaviour, bullies and victims. You can pick and choose questions from these lists to meet you own requirements.

About 10 to 12 questions should be enough.

Answer the questions to find out among other things:

+ What your attitudes are towards bullying.

+ Who is being bullied in your family?

+ What type of bullying takes place?

+ Who the bullies are.

+ What do you think bullying is?

+ How you perceive bullying is dealt with in the family?

Section 1

QUESTIONNAIRES FOR PARENTS: RELATED TO SCHOOL

1. In what ways do you think children can be bullied?

2. Why do you think that some children, rather than others, are bullies?

3. Why do you think that some children, rather than others, are bullied?

4. Have your children ever been bullied?

5. Why do you think that they were bullied?

6. What did you do about it and what was the result of your action?

7. Can we sometimes ignore bullying?

8. Have you observed any bullying during the past two weeks?

9. Where did it happen?

10. What happened?

11. Did you do anything to stop it?

12. If yes, what did you do?

13. If you did not, why not?

14. Has your child been involved in any bullying?

15. What did you do about?

16. What do you advise your child to do if he/she is being bullied?

17. Is the school the type of school where you can report bullying?

18. Where does most bullying take place in the school?

19. Is enough being done to stop bullying in the school?

20. What more do you think could be done?

21. If we were all to do one thing in our school to reduce bullying, what do you think that should be?

Thank you for filling in this questionnaire.

Section 2

A QUESTIONNAIRE FOR PARENTS: WHY DO CHILDREN BULLY?

If you suspect that your child is engaged in bullying you must first of all try to work out the reasons for the behaviour and these will point you towards resolving the problem.

The reasons for children bullying can come from a variety of areas.

List from 1 to 10 *in order of importance* the following reasons for children bullying:

1.   They are jealous of other children.

       _____

2.   They want to get attention and show off in front of others.

       _____

3.   They are told to do it by other bullies and they bully so as not to be left out and to prove themselves.

       _____

4.   For some reason they enjoy humiliating, hurting and making others miserable.

       _____

5.   They are being bullied by others and want some revenge.

       _____

6.   They do not have a sense of being fair and they are bad losers.

       _____

7. Bossing others and shoving them around makes them feel good.

    _____

8. They are not used to taking turns and sharing and they always want their own way.

    _____

9. They are disturbed and need help from doctors or others.

    _____

10. They feel bad about themselves and they take it out on others.

    _____

11. They find it difficult to make, or keep, friends.

    _____

12. There is a lot of bullying in the children's home.

    _____

13. They cannot feel or see other people's pain when they hurt them.

    _____

14. They believe that strong people should dominate and bully weaker people.

    _____

15. They feel picked on in the home, at play and at school and they are angry.

    _____

16. They enjoy bullying and they know that they will get away with it.

_____

17. They have not been told or, if they have, they do not clearly understand, that bullying is not acceptable in the home.

_____

18. Bullying is their way of frightening others and showing their power.

_____

19. They cannot enjoy other people's successes in class or at games.

_____

Thank you for filling in this questionnaire.

Section 3

A QUESTIONNAIRE ON BULLYING IN GENERAL

Please read these statements about bullying and think about them. Then rank 10 of them *in order of importance.*

Place the numbers 1 to 10 beside the ones you choose as most important in terms of bullying as you see it. We can talk about some of these statements later if you wish.

1. We can bully others through our actions, words and gestures.

   _____

2. A bully takes pleasure in hurting others and humiliating them.

   _____

3. Bullies are clever and do most of their work in secret.

   _____

4. We should never criticise a bully in public. He/she will only become worse.

   _____

5. Bullies only think of themselves.

   _____

6. Bullies always feel bad about themselves.

   _____

7. If we beat or strike people who bully others, they may think that their own behaviour was correct.

   _____

8.   Too much bullying behaviour goes un-checked in society.

_____

9.   Aggressive parents are responsible for agg-ressive children.

_____

10. A bully can be a bully because of his/her experience in life.

_____

11. Bullies are always to blame for their be-haviour.

_____

12. Victims must never feel guilty because they have been bullied.

_____

13. Only strong people bully.

_____

14. Bullying can create major problems for people.

_____

15. Bullying affects your ability to learn.

_____

16. If you are strong, you should help those who are weak.

_____

17. If you are being bullied, you should tell someone, or you are helping the bully.

_____

18. Bullies often need help and advice them-
     selves.

     _____

19. Bullies choose who to pick on.

     _____

20. All bullies are unpopular and have few
     friends.

     _____

21. It is not a sign of weakness to ask for
     help.

     _____

22. Bullying sometimes is allowed to con-
     tinue because we do not tell the people
     who should be told.

     _____

23. Every kind of bullying is equally bad.

     _____

24. Sometimes we have to avoid bullies.

     _____

25. Bullying is undeserved by victims and
     they have a right to seek help.

     _____

26. Name-calling is really not bullying.

     _____

27. We should help others if they are being
     bullied.

     _____

28. Bullies love us to keep bullying a secret.

     _____

29. Bullies make people do things for them through fear.

    _____

30. People of every age can bully or be bullied.

    _____

Thank you for filling in this questionnaire.

Section 4

AN AWARENESS-RAISING QUESTIONNAIRE ON BULLYING

This is an exercise in raising awareness of and finding out about bullying. There are 21 questions/statements listed below. You will probably decide not to use them all, depending on what is happening with your children, or in your home.

Read the statements listed below and write in *true* or *false* after each.

1.   Some people who are annoying deserve to be bullied.

      _____

2.   Only children bully others.

      _____

3.   Boys bully as much as girls.

      _____

4.   Bullying toughens you up and helps you deal with life.

      _____

5.   When you isolate someone and get others to join you in doing it you are bullying.

      _____

6.   The best way to treat a bully is to give him/her a taste of their own medicine.

      _____

7.   Parents who bully give bad messages to
      their children.

      _____

8.   When we are picked on, we isolate our-
      selves and feel bad about ourselves.

      _____

9.   Most bullying in school takes place in the
      playground.

      _____

10.   There is a difference between rough play
      and bullying.

      _____

11.   Bullying is part of growing up. It is good
      for you.

      _____

12.   All bullies are big and strong and rough.

      _____

13.   Nobody deserves to be bullied or should
      allow themselves to be bullied.

      _____

14.   There is always someone to tell if you
      are being bullied.

      _____

15.   You are weak and ought to be ashamed
      if you have to go and ask for help if you
      are being bullied.

      _____

16.   It is good to talk to someone and ask for
      help if you need it.

      _____

17.   We must not allow bullying or bullies to hide in our families or communities.

_____

18.   Every child has a right to be happy and to be allowed to learn.

_____

19.   Some children are bullied because others are jealous of them.

_____

20.   Bullies are not popular in their families, communities, classes or schools.

_____

21.   Bullies cannot think of others because they are so wrapped up in themselves.

_____

Thank you for filling in this questionnaire.

GENERAL POINTS RELATING
TO THE QUESTIONNAIRES

When we are asking for *true* or *false* answers, most of the questions or statements are not clear-cut.

There may be some ambivalent attitudes among parents around bullying (e.g. everyone is bullied at sometime and you have to put up with it; my Dad said that he was bullied and it never did him any harm), which you may gently tease out.

Many issues can arise and much useful information can be elicited which will give direction for strategies which can be used in tackling bullying and ensuring that we do our best to protect our children from being preyed on by bullies or engaging in bullying behaviour.

Appendix 2

Recommended Booklist

B Byrne, *Bullying: A Community Approach* (Dublin: Columba Press) 1994.

B Byrne, *Coping with Bullying in Schools* (Dublin: Columba Press) 1993. This is an excellent book.

INTO, *Enhancing Self-esteem* (Dublin: INTO Publications) 1995.

V & CAB O'Donnell, *Bullying: A Resource Guide for Teachers and Parents* (Dublin: Attic Press) 1995.

D Olweus, *Bullying at School: What we know and what we can do* (Oxford: Blackwell Publishers) 1993.

R Pianta & D Walsh, *High Risk Children in Schools* (New York/London: Routledge) 1996.

K Rigby, *Bullying in Schools and what to do about it* (London: Kingsley) 1997.

E Roland & E Munthe, *Bullying: An International Perspective* (London: Fulton) 1989.

S Skynner & J Cleese, *Families and How to Survive them* (UK: Cedar) 1983.

P K Smith & G S Sharp (eds), *School Bullying: Insights and Perspectives* (London/New York: Routledge) 1995.

G Stenhouse, *Developing your Child's Self-esteem* (Oxford: Oxford University Press) 1994.

D P Tattum, *Understanding and Managing Bullying* (London: Heinemann) 1993.

A Train, *The Bullying Problem* (UK: Souvenir Press) 1995. This is an excellent book.

S B Turkel & S Eth, "Psycho-pathological Response to Stress" in Arnold, *Childhood Stress* (New York: Wiley) 1990.